Cha

01
The Conversation

02
Shaping Identity through Relationships

03
Battlefield of the Mind

04
Feelings Lie

05
Perception vs Reality

06
Life Interrupted

07
Embracing Truth & Overcoming Loneliness

08
The Unveiling of Truth

09
Walking in Truth

Dedication

This book is for the 11-year-old girl that stayed hidden for years in this adult body. I want to take this time to tell you what I didn't have the courage to say back then

I love you and you are worth it

A Letter To You

When I first decided to write this book, I was battling exactly what God wanted to do through it. I was going back and forth because it was not naturally easy for me to talk about myself. I spoke to God and told him, I don't think I can do this, this is your plan but I don't believe I'm the right person for the job. That same night I went to bed and received a message from God in my sleep. He said, "You put pen to paper, and I'll provide the content."

In the season I was in, I didn't know just what to speak about, I later realized my fear was in my mask falling off and being exposed to the very world which I've always tried to hide from. Understand that in this season I had been exposed to people by people, therefore, I wanted to hold every ounce of dignity I had left. People pleasing, I found, wasn't my only problem, rather having the strength to walk confidently in who I was regardless of what others thought of me and my past.

The Holy Spirit directed me greatly as I was writing, but at the same time, the Lord was breaking me down on the inside. I realized I had entered a season of transformation. This book is not just for others, it is an intricate part of my very own deliverance. I pray that this book will Bless all that take the time to read. It's not about the exposure it's about recognizing your truth and learning how to walk confidently in it!

Beautiful Chaos was birth out of a place of full surrender to God. It wasn't until I went through a season of solitude that I really begin to understand exactly what a full surrender really meant. The only thing that I can do in order for you to truly understand what this amazing transformation process was like, is to be as honest as I can be regarding my experiences. It is my hope and prayer that as you read you can begin to examine yourself. I had to understand, and I hope that it resonates with you as well, there is a process to healing that teaches us the truth in finding ourselves, and what that means as it relates to our call.

Just. T

CHAPTER ONE

The Conversation

While sitting in the park, engaged in a conversation with my friend, a profound realization struck me like a bolt of lightning. This exchange had become a turning point, a pivotal moment that would shape my future in unforeseen ways. To truly grasp the significance of this moment, I must first provide some context about my friend.

She possessed a rare gift of unfiltered honesty, always saying what she meant and meaning what she said. Although her forthrightness sometimes proved challenging, I valued her ability to see beyond facades and dig deep into the core of a person. Unbeknownst to me, our conversation that day would unravel layers of my soul, exposing truths I had long kept hidden.

We delved into my personal fears and the raw emotions surrounding my departure from a church I had faithfully attended for years. The rejection I felt from those I held dear had caused me immense pain, as I struggled to reconcile their carelessness with the spiritual guidance I sought. It wasn't that I couldn't understand the hurt I may have caused with my decisions; rather, it was the absence of empathetic guidance from my church leaders that pushed me away. I yearned for someone who could comprehend my journey and walk alongside me, empowered by the Holy Spirit.

"Healing happens when you say yes to the process of the unknown"
Just T

Throughout our conversation, I repeatedly asserted that most people couldn't handle me. This belief had become deeply ingrained within me, prompting the construction of impenetrable walls to keep others at bay. I carefully presented only what I wanted the world to see, leaving the rest to their imagination. Strangely, with this particular friend, I found myself instinctively opening up, allowing her into the protective fortress I had built. The ease with which I shared my vulnerabilities with her frightened me, yet deep down, I recognized the accuracy of her observations about me.

During that conversation, an epiphany washed over me. It dawned on me that my struggle was not with people per se, but with the pain of rejection itself. Now, I understand that you might think, "Who hasn't faced rejection and had to overcome it?" Undoubtedly, many of you reading this book have experienced rejection and understand the profound anguish it can inflict. However, I want to offer a spiritual perspective on this universal human experience.

Like so many others, I had allowed rejection to penetrate my soul deeply. Continually losing friends, feeling like the perpetual outsider, and lacking lasting relationships led me to question my own worth. I was plagued by self-doubt and a relentless belief that something was inherently wrong with me. Memories of childhood bullying and the cruel labels thrust upon me played on an endless loop in my mind, gradually eroding my self-esteem. The fight against rejection, I soon discovered, was not primarily about others' opinions; it was about how I perceived myself despite those opinions or actions.

In my desperate quest for acceptance, I sought to mold myself into what others desired, perpetually conforming to their expectations. Whether it was assimilating into popular circles through basketball or embracing my nerdy inclinations alongside computer-savvy friends, I constantly sought a place where I could belong. Yet, deep down, I knew that these adaptations were a façade—a desperate attempt to avoid further rejection.

The rejection I faced within the church community was especially painful. As my second church home, it felt like a devastating blow. Experiencing rejection from fellow churchgoers and even pastors weighed heavily on my heart. I had anticipated finding acceptance and support in a spiritual haven, only to be cast aside once again.

Reflecting on my journey, I began to discern the patterns that shaped my response to rejection. Childhood memories of bullying and being labeled had left indelible scars, causing me to question my intrinsic worth. The opinions and actions of others further fueled these negative beliefs about myself.

> *"If it tears you up on the inside, you have got to get it out. Talk to someone before it kills you"*
>
> *-Just T*

In an effort to break free from the shackles of rejection, I embarked on a journey of self-discovery and healing. I knew it would be an arduous path, but I also understood that God's love and grace surpassed any rejection I had faced.

With renewed determination, I immersed myself in God's Word, seeking to comprehend His unconditional love and acceptance. I surrounded myself with a community of believers who offered unwavering support and encouragement, journeying alongside me as I confronted my deep-rooted insecurities. I discovered that the more I aligned my identity with God's truth, the less power others' opinions held over me.

Gradually, I learned to embrace my uniqueness and view rejection as an opportunity for growth rather than a reflection of my worth. I realized that rejection was not a measure of my value but a redirection toward the people and places where I genuinely belonged.

Throughout this transformative journey, I not only found healing from past wounds but also cultivated a deeper intimacy with God. In His presence, I discovered His love was constant, unwavering, and independent of my performance or the opinions of others. The acceptance and belonging my heart yearned for, I found in Him.

As my conversation with my friend at the park drew to a close, I felt a renewed sense of hope and purpose. The pain of rejection had served as a catalyst for transformation, unearthing a profound understanding of my identity. No longer defined by the fear of rejection, I embraced the truth of who I was in Christ.

From that transformative moment forward, I resolved to live fully in the identity of a beloved child of God. His acceptance proved more than sufficient. As I continued my journey, I discovered that my story of overcoming rejection could serve as a wellspring of encouragement and inspiration for others wrestling with similar struggles.

Little did I know that this pivotal conversation would mark the inception of a new chapter in my life—a chapter brimming with healing, growth, and a profound sense of belonging in the embrace of a loving God.

Chapter Takeaways

Chapter Takeaways

Affirmations

I am mentally well and stable.

I am in the process of healing my mental health for good.

I am choosing to focus on mental wellness.

My diagnosis was the starting point to build a better life.

I will replace my negative thoughts with positive thoughts.

I become more and more grateful for life each day that I wake up.

I deserve a life filled with happiness and love.

I prioritize and practice self-care on the daily basis.

Scripture Reference

Philippians 4:13

I can do all things through him who strengthens me.

CHAPTER TWO

Shaping Identity Through Relationships

Relationships are a huge part of our lives whether we want people in our lives or not. We will forever have to deal with relationships.

Relationships weave themselves into the tapestry of our lives, whether we embrace their presence or not. They hold immense power to mold our very being. It was during my first year of middle school that I began to grasp the profound significance of these organic connections. Family, friends, acquaintances, teachers—their influence left an indelible mark on my journey. Among them, however, stood Janet, my first verified bully, whose impact surpassed all others.

On a crisp autumn morning, my day unfolded swiftly, a rhythm I cherished. The school's academic environment thrilled me, yet its luster was tarnished by social cliques dictating the who, what, when, and why of every student. Learning often played second fiddle to the ceaseless quest of my peers to fit into these groups. So, I eagerly awaited the end of each day, seeking solace in my own solitude. A quiet, introverted type, I diligently completed my tasks and relished the guidance of my teachers. But as you might imagine, my peers didn't take kindly to my earnestness. I was labeled the goody two shoes or the teacher's pet.

One particular morning, I found myself fixated on the clock, anticipating the next class. Positioned in the front row, directly in front of the projector, I absorbed the teacher's lessons. Clad in baggy blue jeans and a generous green sweater from the thrift store, my unique attire deviated from the fashion norms of the time. To aid my hearing, I wore a pair of bulky headphones connected to a small microphone adorning my teacher's shirt. The microphone transmitted her amplified voice directly into my ears. After enduring periods of hearing impairment, the clarity was akin to heaven. Immersed in my studies, I remained focused—an easy task since I lacked a sizable circle of friends.

The class proceeded as usual. I jotted down the homework assignment while the teacher lectured. Suddenly, a sharpened pencil whizzed through the air, striking my face with a painful impact. The entire class erupted in laughter. Stunned, I glanced up just in time to catch Janet's triumphant smile from two desks ahead. To this day, I cannot fathom why I became her chosen target for bullying. I had never provoked trouble or sought conflict. I preferred solitude, keeping my head down.

Silence became my shield, my defense against such torment from my peers. I believed that if I avoided bothering them, they would reciprocate and leave me alone. However, I soon discovered that reality doesn't always align with our hopes. That evening, as I returned home, my spirit lay in ruins. Tears streamed down my face for what felt like hours. My strategy had failed. People witnessed my pain, my hurt, my embarrassment. It felt as though my world was crumbling. I'm not one to indulge in theatrics, but this ordeal would have appeared dramatic to any observer. What must be understood is that I prided myself on being unseen. It wasn't the act of bullying itself that troubled me, as one might assume, but rather the audacity of someone breaching my walls, casting unwanted attention upon me.

The bullying persisted throughout the year, and I endured it silently. Though it never escalated to physical violence, the relentless torment chipped away at my mental fortitude. At that tender age, I struggled to comprehend the lesson this experience was meant to impart. Even then, I recognized that everything happens for a reason, but this particular instance defied any logical explanation. The bullying shaped my self-perception and colored my understanding of relationships.

Janet's words seemed to reflect the thoughts of everyone else. Her hurtful remarks held tremendous power because I internalized them, unwittingly embracing the distorted narrative she wove. The incessant name-calling, reminders of my disabilities, and instances where she ruthlessly mocked my very existence shaped my self-image. I failed to realize that I was perpetuating a lie—adopting others' opinions as my own. It didn't define who I truly was.

In that pivotal stage of self-discovery, my experiences carved the path of my existence, regardless of my intentions. I lacked the spiritual maturity to navigate such trials, for I hadn't yet forged a relationship with God. Unaware of His intentions, I began to believe the fabricated tales derived from these experiences. In essence, if I was made to feel inferior based on what someone told me, I would continue to internalize and echo that falsehood. Thus, I unwittingly transformed it into my reality, and my life adapted accordingly.

We are what we constantly consume, a concept echoed both in spiritual teachings. Whether we feed on the word of God or the scientific principles that govern our desires, the underlying truth remains consistent. Consider the saying "you are what you eat." It applies not only to physical nourishment but also to the thoughts and beliefs we internalize. Truth or falsehood, repeated exposure molds our reality. I began responding to the person I believed I was. If others deemed me insignificant, how could I expect to form meaningful connections, friendships, or even find a romantic partner? This flawed thinking tormented me to the point that whenever someone sought to build a relationship with me, I remained guarded, constantly questioning their motives.

Relationships hold profound significance in our human experience, and the wounds inflicted by others can drive us to isolate ourselves from the very connections we need. We were born to forge relationships, an innate desire that aligns with God's intentions. His unyielding love, ever-present and unwavering, serves as a testament to this truth. Despite our flaws and missteps, His love remains constant.

Yet, for me, disappointment often arose from the inability of human relationships to mirror that divine love. Within the scriptures, we encounter numerous accounts of Jesus and His relationships. Sometimes I ponder why Jesus would willingly connect with flawed beings like us when we continually fall short. Here we are, created by Him and from Him, yet we do everything in our power to avoid the very thing He desires most—a relationship.

Indeed, a relationship with Jesus offers unparalleled revelations. Paradoxically, this is what many of us shy away from—the profound identity found in Christ. I, too, struggled to recognize the person Jesus described when He spoke of me. His words contradicted my deeply ingrained beliefs.

"You become what you choose to focus on"

Chapter Takeaways

Chapter Takeaways

Affirmations

I love myself and my flaws while working towards becoming a better person.

I only treat myself with the utmost compassion, kindness, and love.

My mental health diagnosis and issues do not define who I am as a person.

I am creating better mental health each and every day.

I fall more in love with who I am each day.

I am unafraid to share my true feelings.

My life is filled with positive people and things.

Scripture Reference

Deuteronomy 31:6

Be strong and courageous. Do not fear or be in dread of them, for it is the Lord your God who goes with you. He will not leave you or forsake you.

CHAPTER THREE

Battlefield of the Mind

Throughout this book, I will continually revisit incidents and stories from the Bible that have helped me gain a deeper understanding of myself. I found myself in a state of turmoil, primarily due to my aspirations, the person I longed to become, and my inability to attain it.

Is it foolish thinking or not?

We often hear preachers cautioning us about the perils of wrong thinking. Joyce Meyer dedicated an entire series to this topic alone, titled "The Battlefield of the Mind." What exactly is this battlefield she speaks of? Why is it so significant that many emphasize its importance? Well, in simple terms, our minds are the playground of the devil. At least, that's how my mother used to describe it. It is the battleground where he excels, as he consistently employs the same tactics and we often fall victim to them.

When I refer to the enemy, it is important to understand that he is also a spirit who is well-versed in the ways of God, just as we should be. He has walked with God and had a relationship with Him. Therefore, he knows the ways of God well enough to employ that knowledge in his battle against us in our minds. The enemy understands that if he can win the battle within our minds, he can turn us against ourselves. No, he doesn't directly soil his hands; instead, he manipulates us into playing into our own downfall.

> "The enemy knows if he can win the battle in our minds, he can play us against ourselves. No, he does not get his hands dirty; instead, he helps you to play yourself."

Our experiences often shape our perception of reality. It is common for most of us to question whether we deserve the trauma or pain we encounter. This is where many people find themselves at odds with God because they struggle to comprehend how a loving God can permit certain things to happen. The world will perpetually grapple with this issue because numerous opinions exist on the matter.

As I matured, my guard grew alongside me. I became cautious in my interactions and scrutinized every relationship I encountered. To put it plainly, I entered protective mode. Due to a lack of trust in people, I felt the need to shield myself. Years passed after that dreadful year of being bullied, but healing eluded me. In fact, I wasn't even aware that I needed healing. Instead, I began to develop a hardened exterior.

By the time I turned thirteen, I had already experienced several unwelcome sexual encounters. I share this briefly because I want to empower young women who may be battling such situations at present, as well as the mothers who still need healing themselves but must be there for their daughters. These experiences are precisely what prey on the mind.

Ultimately, it all boils down to one's sense of worth. Sex carries numerous meanings and interpretations that arise from our experiences and beliefs. When we hold ourselves in low esteem, we are more likely to accept situations that provide us with the validation we desperately seek. This holds great significance in the life of a young woman. She must navigate the thought process of giving herself to someone, knowing there is a risk of not getting it right the first time. However, in youth, the focus often centers on the present moment and what it can offer. These experiences, regardless of the extent of sexual involvement, would forever change me.

The context in which I speak, I believe, can be comprehended by those who are drawn to pick up this book. While we often hear stories about unwanted sexual experiences in youth, particularly concerning young girls, we rarely delve into the mindset of these young girls. Instead, we are frequently judged and ridiculed for decisions that are misunderstood. I will never advocate for engaging in sexual relations before one is emotionally and mentally mature enough, and in a committed relationship. However, I was that girl who made a decision that would ultimately shape my perception of sex and people. At the time, I failed to realize how much I was playing into the hands of the enemy. He wasn't just after me; he was after my mind.

One warm summer day, I, along with many other neighborhood kids, were running, playing, and spending time together. Our meeting spot was always in front of my house. With so many children around, there wasn't much opportunity for one-on-one interactions. However, despite this, I found myself in an extremely uncomfortable position before I was truly ready, all because of my desire to have a relationship. Allow me to pause for a moment and clarify that I offer no excuses for the decisions I made. I simply want the reader to be open to understanding that many of my choices were influenced by my experiences, my longing for friendships, and my need to please those in my life in order to maintain their presence. Looking back on this, I now realize that these events nurtured the people-pleasing mindset that I began to develop, all in the pursuit of satisfying my need for relationships.

I know that I am not alone in this process of seeking to please others during my youth. We do it to seek validation. God has created us with a natural inclination to depend on Him, which highlights the significance of relationships, especially our relationship with Him. I will delve deeper into this topic in a later chapter. For now, I want to emphasize the origin of this desire for relationships. We were created with this need because we were designed to be in relationship with others. However, we often taint these relationships and place blame on God when they don't unfold as we had hoped.

On that particular day, everything seemed normal, except for the conversation I had with him, my first friend, the previous night, which replayed relentlessly in my mind. He was a boy I had met during the summer, visiting his family in our neighborhood. We spent a lot of time together, and I quickly grew fond of him. What made me like him even more was the fact that he wasn't from my area, so he was not influenced by the preconceived opinions others held of me. He got to know the real me, and he still liked me.

We flirted throughout the summer, never making concrete plans. After all, I knew I wasn't ready for the discussions we were having. Being older and more experienced, he persuaded me that having a sexual encounter with him would solidify our relationship. We would be together, despite the physical distance separating us. This act would demonstrate our commitment to each other.

By the end of our conversation, I found myself agreeing to something I didn't truly want to do. I was afraid that if I said no, the news would spread, and I would once again face humiliation similar to the day the pencil was thrown in my face. I couldn't bear another public embarrassment, so I complied.

I hesitated throughout the ordeal, torn by the knowledge that what was happening was not right. Silently, I prayed to God, even up until the moment that boy touched me, begging for His intervention. I didn't want to be there, I didn't want to go through with it, but I didn't know how to stop it. At least, that's what I convinced myself. I knew that if I were to resist, there was a good chance he would turn against me as well. Consequently, I went along with it and experienced my first unwanted sexual encounter.

He interpreted my reluctance as inexperience, but in reality, I was scared, desperately wishing for God to rescue me. And indeed, God did just that. During the course of that experience, we were caught red-handed by one of his family members who promptly spread the news. We had to quickly compose ourselves and pretend as if nothing had transpired. We managed to escape consequences, but our relationship was forever changed.

I sensed a level of anger in him that I had never witnessed before. Seeking clarity, I called him that evening, and our conversation was brief but revealing. He directed his anger towards me, accusing me of wasting time by debating instead of readily acquiescing to his desires. He felt played, as if I had led him on. In my attempt to explain the internal struggle I had faced, he cursed at me and abruptly hung up. I never heard from him again.

Rejection can manifest in various forms. In this case, I was suddenly dismissed by the person I had been pursuing all summer. The battle of my self-worth took center stage in my mind. For weeks afterward, I experienced constant regret, humiliation, anger, and a host of other emotions. Most profoundly, I felt the sting of rejection from someone I believed I had built a genuine connection with. I firmly believed that regardless of the circumstances, I was secure in his friendship. Only afterward did I realize that I had made a decision to be with a boy who I knew would be leaving, yet in my mind, I had convinced myself that I meant the world to him. Despite our limitations, I believed we would be forever friends.

We often fail to grasp the long-term consequences of our decisions, especially when we are young. The weight of each choice is grossly underestimated. That was certainly the case for me when it came to sex. I didn't fully comprehend how much I valued it. In my mind, it represented the ultimate surrender of oneself to another, a bond that couldn't be broken or tarnished by anyone. If I were to give myself to another person, it was because I had complete confidence in their ability to fulfill my every need. It never occurred to me that I was just a child, lacking the emotional capacity to handle the complexities that come with sex. To this day, I still define it in much the same way.

Our minds are the playground of the enemy. What a uniquely perfect opportunity for an example. The enemy knew my weakness, but he also understood how I was created. I not only needed relationships, but I had an intense longing for them. What better way to lead me towards self-destruction than by convincing me that it was only about sex? He persuaded me that I had no other choice but to fulfill the expectations placed upon me because I needed this relationship. After all, it's not as if friends were knocking on my door.

The enemy's primary tactic to keep us in a state of defeat is to maintain a negative mindset. My experiences could either make me stronger or crush me—it all depended on what I chose to believe. Remember, when I mentioned earlier that the enemy doesn't fight fair? Well, I should have clarified that the enemy cannot defeat you in a battle unless you allow him to. His ability to harm you is contingent upon your cooperation.

Experiences Could Either Make Me Stronger or Defeat Me

Chapter Takeaways

Chapter Takeaways

Affirmations

Starting my day with gratitude fills me with positive vibes and improves my mood.

All of my emotional and mental states are in balance and harmony.

As I nourish my mind with happy, healthy thoughts, I ward off stress and anxiety.

I release all emotional blockages that are preventing me from enjoying peace of mind.

I free my mind of all the <u>negative thoughts</u> that keep holding me back.

I heal my mind and make peace with my past by letting go of anger, guilt, resentment, and regret.

I disconnect myself from thoughts and feelings that hinder my self-esteem, sense of self-worth, and overall well-being.

Today I am shifting from a negative to a positive mindset so I can attract all the good things the universe has in store for me.

Scripture Reference

Isaiah 40:31

But they who wait for the Lord shall renew their strength; they shall mount up with wings like eagles; they shall run and not be weary; they shall walk and not faint.

CHAPTER FOUR

Feelings Lie

Our Mind is our Central Intelligence Agency

Our mind is the central intelligence agency of our being. It is the repository of our experiences, shaping our actions, words, and processes. The decisions we make are products of this agency, controlling our thoughts and guiding our behavior. That's why it is crucial for us to have control over what we allow into our minds, including the people and voices that surround us.

In my journey, I faced the challenge of a hearing impairment from a young age. Wearing hearing aids made me a target for ridicule and picking on by my classmates throughout grade school. The lack of understanding among children my age led to hurtful comments that shaped my perception of myself. Unfortunately, I internalized those words and let them define me, not realizing the damage I was inflicting upon myself. It wasn't just about what others said to me; it was about what I allowed myself to repeat.

I repeated exposure to certain thoughts and beliefs can mold them into our truth. I called those hurtful words poison because they formed a false opinion of who I was and who I was destined to be. Consequently, I couldn't fully embrace the truth of what God, my creator, said about me. I questioned how God could call me blessed with the limitations I had to live with, and why He would put me in a position to be picked on because of my impairment. These questions stemmed from a limited mindset, one that only saw the negative.

It took time for me to realize how much I had been affected by my own words, regardless of their source. People might assume that because I graduated early, acquired multiple degrees, and established a successful company, I overcame those negative thoughts. However, the truth is that I still struggle daily with feelings of inadequacy and limitation. I had to actively retrain my thoughts in order to become the person I am today.

Changing our mindset is a critical endeavor, regardless of our current circumstances, if we wish to elevate ourselves in any area of life. The opinions of friends, cultural influences, family, and past experiences should not restrict us from fulfilling our true potential. Each one of us has a unique path laid out, and no one else can accomplish what God has ordained for us. No one else can touch the lives of the people we were called to impact. There is inherent beauty in our existence, and when we recognize that, we must fight with an unwavering determination. And the battleground lies within our own minds.

Breaking the belief that we are at the mercy of a formidable enemy is not easy. The truth is, the enemy has no power over us except for what we allow him to have. We often fall into the trap of not realizing when we are being influenced. Take, for example, the situation with Janet, who intentionally harmed me emotionally. While she didn't physically hurt me, her actions affected my emotions and feelings, causing me to build walls and distance myself from others who had nothing to do with her actions. Consequently, I may have missed out on opportunities to cultivate healthy relationships because I was nursing my hurt feelings.

What did I do with those hurt feelings? I dwelled on them, allowing them to fester and poison my mind. Unbeknownst to me, the enemy was manipulating my thoughts about people, myself, and my future based on the negative experiences I had. While I remained mad and upset, the enemy reveled in the fact that he could make a single move and I would unknowingly destroy my own life. His most potent weapon is manipulation, using our experiences to sway our decisions based on faulty realities.

In the Bible, God warns us about the mysteries of our own hearts. Jeremiah 17:9-10, in the message version, elucidates this:

"The heart is hopelessly dark and deceitful, a puzzle that no one can figure out. But I, God, search the heart and examine the mind. I get to the heart of the human. I get to the root of things. I treat them as they really are, not as they pretend to be."

This passage reminds us that our hearts and minds can be complex and easily deceived. We may deceive ourselves by pretending to be fine or unaffected by negative experiences, but deep down, the impact lingers, affecting our thoughts, emotions, and decisions.

In order to break free from this cycle of self-deception and manipulation, we must confront our thoughts and beliefs head-on. We must recognize that we have the power to choose what we allow into our minds and what we believe about ourselves and our circumstances.

One powerful tool we have at our disposal is the practice of mindfulness. Mindfulness involves being present in the moment, observing our thoughts and emotions without judgment. By cultivating mindfulness, we can become more aware of the negative thoughts and beliefs that arise within us.

Once we become aware of these negative thoughts, we can challenge them. We can question their validity and examine the evidence supporting them. Often, we will find that these thoughts are based on limited perspectives or past experiences that no longer hold true. By challenging these thoughts, we can begin to reframe them and replace them with more empowering and positive beliefs.

Affirmations are another powerful tool for reprogramming our minds. Affirmations are positive statements that we repeat to ourselves regularly. By consistently affirming positive beliefs about ourselves and our abilities, we can gradually shift our mindset and overcome negative self-talk. For example, instead of repeating thoughts like "I am not good enough," we can affirm, "I am capable and worthy of success."

Surrounding ourselves with positive influences is also crucial in our journey of self-discovery and personal growth. We should seek out relationships and communities that uplift and support us, where we can be surrounded by people who believe in our potential and encourage us to pursue our dreams.

It is important to remember that the power to shape our thoughts and beliefs ultimately lies within us. We have the ability to break free from the chains of negativity and self-doubt. By actively choosing empowering thoughts, challenging negative beliefs, practicing mindfulness, and surrounding ourselves with positivity, we can discover the power within us to create the life we desire.

Our minds are powerful agencies that shape our thoughts, beliefs, and actions. To unlock our true potential, we must be mindful of the thoughts we allow into our minds and challenge negative beliefs. By doing so, we can reframe our thinking, cultivate positive affirmations, and surround ourselves with positive influences. Through these practices, we can discover the power within us to overcome limitations, embrace our true selves, and live a fulfilling and purposeful life.

Chapter Takeaways

Chapter Takeaways

Affirmations

I am in control of my thoughts and will always choose to see the positive in every situation.

I love what I see when I look in the mirror.

I love my belly because it allows me to eat and keeps me healthy.

I trust my body to tell me everything it needs in perfect time.

My body is wise, and I trust its ability to eliminate pain and heal itself.

I am making amazing decisions about what I eat and drink.

Scripture Reference

Isaiah 41:10

Fear not, for I am with you; be not dismayed, for I am your God; I will strengthen you, I will help you, I will uphold you with my righteous right hand.

CHAPTER FIVE

Perception vs Reality

"I was an adult but I was still carrying around a little hurt girl inside of me"

When I graduated from high school and moved to Florida with my family, I was filled with excitement and anticipation. This new chapter of my life meant freedom, independence, and the opportunity to truly be myself. No longer bound by the expectations and judgments of others, I was eager to explore my own path and live according to my own truth. It was a time of adulting, and I was ready to embrace it wholeheartedly.

However, as reality began to set in, I quickly realized just how unprepared I was for the challenges that lay ahead. I had rushed into adulthood with the belief that I had all the answers, but I soon discovered that I was carrying a lot of emotional baggage from my past. The wounds of the little girl within me still dictated my actions and reactions. She longed to be acknowledged and validated, and her presence was a constant reminder of the pain I needed to shield myself from.

In my journey of self-discovery, I came to understand that our perception of people and relationships is often shaped by our past experiences. Our expectations are formed early on, based on the way we define relationships and how we expect to be treated within them. However, this definition fails to take into account the complexities of the unlearned heart and the battles that rage within our minds, affecting not only ourselves but also others.

Recognizing this truth was a pivotal moment for me. As I delved deeper into understanding myself, I couldn't help but consider how many others may not embark on this journey of self-discovery. This path requires intentionality, a willingness to look in the mirror and examine the root of who we are. And in that process, we come to realize that our true identity can only be found in the One who created us. This realization changes everything, shaping the way we view ourselves and others.

While I didn't grow up in a church environment, my mother would occasionally take us to different churches when I was younger. I witnessed the diversity of denominations, from Pentecostal to Baptist, and wondered why there were so many different ways of worshiping the one God we all served.

However, my experiences with organized religion often left me feeling disconnected. I yearned for a personal connection with God, but I found religion to be a barrier. I sought a closeness to God that went beyond the confines of man-made systems.

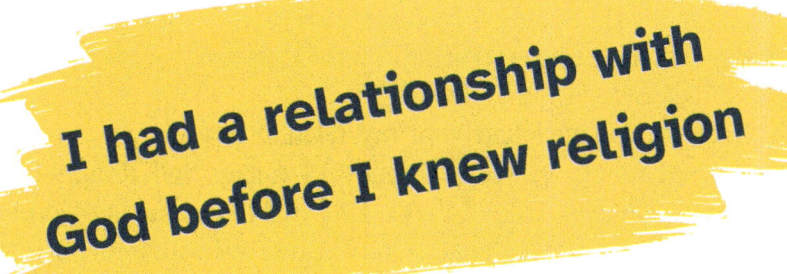

I had a relationship with God before I knew religion

During my time working the overnight shift at a nursing home, I formed bonds with my co-workers who became like a second family to me. In the midst of the job's challenges, these women provided a safe space for me to be myself. Known for my straightforwardness, I openly discussed my thoughts on religion and my relationship with God. Many couldn't fully comprehend my viewpoints, but I no longer felt the need to convince anyone of my personal connection with the Holy Spirit—I simply lived it.

One night, as we sat outside during a break, engaged in a deep discussion about death, a friend shared her fear of losing her son, prompted by a vivid dream she had. In the midst of our heightened emotions, a Christian nurse joined the conversation. She asked if anyone in the group had not yet given their life to Christ. Fear gripped us all, as there was a sense of recognition that God might be sending a warning, even if we didn't fully understand the dream's meaning.

Reluctantly, I raised my hand, trembling with a battle raging inside me. On one hand, I desired to publicly dedicate my life to God, to fully live for Him. On the other hand, I feared failure and the potential rejection that might follow. This fear stemmed from a pattern that had haunted me since middle school—the fear of being exposed and not being accepted for who I truly was.

Up until that point, I had kept my relationship with God private, shielding myself from the possibility of falling and disappointing others. Yet, I finally realized that if I wanted to live the life God had destined for me, I had to let go of that young girl within me. She had to die so that I could truly live as the person God intended me to be. I had been called to do great things, but I could only step into that calling by taking control of my thoughts and feelings, and learning to see through spiritual eyes.

God revealed to me that as spiritual beings, we are not of this world but merely foreigners passing through. Trying to operate solely within the confines of this world would limit us. God's analogy struck a chord with me: If you go to a different country and settle down, you can never fully integrate and function there as you would in your own country. Similarly, as spiritual beings in an earthly realm, our language, values, and way of life may seem foreign to those who do not share our faith. They may struggle to comprehend beyond what they see and what they can achieve themselves.

However, when we embrace our identity as spiritual beings on a temporary assignment, we find solace. We realize that the opinions and acceptance of the world are not our ultimate concern. We understand that our actions on earth have eternal significance, and we are not striving for earthly rewards but rather for treasures in the realm of eternity. Even when we stumble and fall, we can rise again because we know that the world, which is foreign to the Spirit, does not dictate our true worth or determine the outcome of our journey.

In embracing my identity as a foreigner to this world, I began to walk in a newfound confidence. The little girl within me, with all her fears and insecurities, gradually faded away. I embarked on a journey of self-discovery and spiritual growth, fully aware that I was called to live a life that might be misunderstood by others. And that was okay because I had found my true identity in the One who created me.

As I closed that chapter of my life and stepped into the unknown, I embraced the foreigner within me. I no longer feared the spotlight or the possibility of rejection. I knew that my purpose was greater than my own limitations, and that as long as I walked hand in hand with God, I would find fulfillment and peace.

The journey was far from over, but I was ready to face the challenges with a newfound perspective. I was no longer held captive by the opinions of others or my own past. I was free to be the person God had created me to be, unapologetically and without fear. And with that newfound freedom, I embarked on the next chapter of my life, eager to see what lay ahead on this extraordinary journey of faith.

Chapter Takeaways

Chapter Takeaways

Affirmations

I have the power to help my body heal and renew without medicine.

I improve my health every day just by having a positive attitude.

I am not what I eat, I am much more than that.

My beautiful skin always shields and protects my body.

I feed my tasty, healthy things that help me remain as healthy as possible.

I love every inch of my body and treat it as such.

I have a strong and healthy immune system that fights off illness.

Scripture Reference

Exodus 15:2

The Lord is my strength and my song, and he has become my salvation; this is my God, and I will praise him, my father's God, and I will exalt him.

CHAPTER SIX
Life Interrupted

Have you ever sat back and thought about all the time that has passed you by? Have you ever had seasons where you can't for the life of you figure out how you got to where you are? So often we dismiss the warning, the plan, the experiences, and proper leading from the Holy Spirit in order to submit to the path that is comfortable and seemingly easy enough to follow.

In reality, though we may not have a plan written down, we still craft these plans in our heads. They may include what we want to do when we grow up, what college to go to, what people you will spend our time with, what career path we will choose, or how many kids we will have. These are plans that are crafted in our own minds to fit our own agenda. We see the future we want and we go for it.

Now don't get me wrong, there is nothing wrong with planning, in fact, without a plan very little gets accomplished. Those who fail to plan often find themselves binge-watching on Netflix. The reality is, there are many times when God intentionally messes up my life plan. And that's a really good thing.

Let's take a look at Joseph, for instance. God really messed up Joseph's life plan. His brothers threw him into a dry well, then sold him into slavery. The wife of his Egyptian master tried to seduce him. When he refused her advances, she turned him over to the Egyptian cops, who then tossed him in prison. He spent years in prison, waiting to be released. I could bet money that Joseph's plan for life did not include jail time. Finally, after many years of painful waiting, God exalted him to the second in command in all of Egypt.

When all was said and done, listen to what Joseph says to his brothers. "Do not fear, for am I in the place of God? As for you, you meant evil against me, but God meant it for good, to bring it about that many people should be kept alive, as they are today." (Genesis 50:19–20)

God messed up Joseph's life plan, and it was a really good thing. He did for Joseph what Joseph could never have done for himself. There was a bigger purpose to be fulfilled. God has interrupted my life on many occasions. All throughout school, I had this dream of being someone important. I didn't know what that would consist of, but I wanted a career that made a major impact, a position where I could influence thousands. Well, let me tell you, God was not in that thought process. First, I didn't know that I needed to consult him. I made my life plans based on my own agenda. I had no specific goals when I started college; I changed my major several times.

During my sophomore year in college, I found out that I would be having my first child. OMG!!?!!! WHAT NOW????? I was a very determined young woman who took on heavy caseloads in school and at work in order to pay for school because my parents were unable to. However, getting pregnant at the age of 18 taught me that I would have to sacrifice and set new goals because my life had been interrupted.

This came with a whole lot of lessons. It came with years of struggle and having to really buckle down and do what I had to do because I was no longer just taking care of myself. I had a life inside of me that God had trusted me with. To raise him properly in order to fulfill God's plan for his life, so that he can be the asset to this world he was created to be.

In the beginning, the thought of having a baby was scary and confusing at the same time. I use the term confusing here because all I ever had in mind was my plans; I wasn't expecting any disruptions. So it was impossible to plan a counterattack. I had to just go with the flow. As I stated earlier, I learned many lessons in this process. I needed help beyond what I could do if I were going to survive, make it, and be successful.

Having my baby at this stage in my life taught me how to lean on God. My life was interrupted because God wanted me to meet him. He wanted my attention. He knew the type of person I was and knew that I was going to try and make it work on my own.

I had to go without finances, go through a series of health problems, and lack the motivation to continue my education for him to get my attention. Talk about Life Interrupted .At the end of that season, I was able to look back on that year and understand exactly why God allowed the things he allowed. It's like waking up from a dream and realizing your reality looks totally different. It wasn't my plans or abilities that would lead me to success; it was God's. Take time and get to know him.

In Jeremiah 29: 11 **"For I know the plans I have for you,"** declares the LORD, **"plans to prosper you and not to harm you, plans to give you hope and a future."**

My future had been predestined, it had been established. The passions I had in me were from God himself. Though I didn't realize it at the time, I was right where God wanted me. I ended up with four college degrees in different areas of study, and God utilized all of them in his plan for me. I got exactly what I desired, but it was by going by His plan and submitting to His will over my own.

Chapter Takeaways

Chapter Takeaways

Affirmations

I will always treat my body with the love, care, and appreciation it deserves.

My body is deserving of love and appreciation at any size.

I am a gorgeous person, inside and out. I do not need validation from others.

-

Scripture Reference

2 Timothy 1:7

For God gave us a spirit not of fear but of power and love and self-control.

CHAPTER SEVEN

Embracing Truth and Overcoming Loneliness

A part of submitting to God's will is the daily process of self-discovery. As I drew closer to Him, His ways began to make more sense to me, allowing me to shift my trust from my own perceptions to the reality found in His word and the messages He spoke to me daily. For far too long, I had relied solely on my own experiences, which often contradicted the person God was calling me to be.

It was during a visit to the doctor's office, on a cold afternoon during my day off, that I confronted the reality of my situation. I had been clinically diagnosed with post-traumatic stress disorder, which led to bouts of depression. As I sat alone in that sterile room, scrolling through Facebook on my phone, the weight of inadequacy and self-doubt began to consume me.

Having an A.D.D. mindset, my thoughts wandered, and I couldn't seem to stop them. Sitting in that chair, facing the bed covered in paper, I realized I didn't want this to be my life. I didn't want to rely on someone else to tell me how I was doing, whether I needed medication, or if I was okay. It felt like surrendering control of my own well-being to someone who only knew me medically. The frustration surged within me, my pulse quickening and my body tensing.

Just as my thoughts threatened to overwhelm me, a short lady with blonde curls, thick glasses, and a serious expression walked into the room, fixing her gaze directly on me. She asked, in a low but direct tone, "Why do you feel you should come off the medicine?" My guard shot up, and I looked at her with squinted eyes, offering a simple response: "Because I want to."

I didn't want her to list all the potential issues I might face if I stopped taking the medication, nor did I want her to dissuade me from my decision. Surprisingly, her approach disarmed me. She acknowledged that it wasn't the best choice but respected my autonomy. In that moment, I began to trust her and the information she provided.

For years, I had grappled with mental health issues that were often dismissed due to the stigma surrounding them. Once again, I found myself harboring a hidden struggle, unwilling to let anyone know about the thorn that plagued me. Depression brought with it a profound sense of loneliness, a feeling many of us experience but rarely admit.

Loneliness is the melancholy that arises from social isolation, a feeling that can make life incredibly challenging. However, I eventually woke up one day and resolved not to let it defeat me. This awakening process guided me to a new understanding. I reframed my perception of loneliness from an issue to an opportunity.

Our perception of our current state or season determines the path we take. How we respond to our circumstances shapes our growth or perpetuates a cycle of defeat. When it came down to it, I had to make the decision about what would influence my life. I recognized that loneliness was an interruption, as God removed people and things from my life that had become my comfort zones—the places I ran to when the going got tough.

If I wanted to make a change, I had to gain a deeper understanding of myself. True growth comes from redefining our natural perception and gaining wisdom through a spiritual lens. What we see with our natural eyes isn't always the truth. At some point, we must let go of our preconceived notions to grasp the reality of our experiences.

I now comprehend that during seasons of loneliness, I should press in and seek God even more fervently. My desire for personal growth intensifies. These seasons become moments of divine preparation for what lies ahead. God keeps His promise and plans prosperity for me. My only requirement is to keep moving forward, not looking to the left or right, but fully trusting that God holds me in His hands and that He has my best interests at heart. There is no place I would rather be.

As my walls of defense came down, I could hear my doctor's words clearly. This gave me an opportunity to help her understand the true reasons behind my desire to stop taking medication. She then communicated the risks involved and offered a step-by-step approach to discontinuing the medication I believed I no longer needed. If I had remained closed off, I would have missed the chance to learn valuable lessons about how my mental health affected every aspect of my life—as a mother, a wife, a minister, and a teacher.

I had to be honest with myself and willing to learn from someone who possessed greater knowledge about mental health. I had to be open to being educated, ensuring my continued well-being and a successful future without relying on medication. Some people enter our lives to provide the information we need to live fulfilling and prosperous lives. We cannot achieve our full potential or positively impact others if we are not receptive to learning, growing, and transforming.

Even to this day, I can only share what I have learned about myself through my own experiences. I don't have all the answers to my own story, but I have discovered that there is still much to be uncovered. As I open myself up more and dissect each experience, I realize that someone greater was and is in control of every aspect of my life. I can now identify when I am bound, shutting down, or excessively focused on my perceptions rather than reality.

Chapter Takeaways

Chapter Takeaways

Affirmations

I have been blessed with great physical health.

Every organ in my body is healthy and functioning as it should.

I nourish my body with healthy foods and vital care because it deserves it.

My body is healing right at this moment. I believe it. I don't have to wait

for the evidence to manifest.

Scripture Reference

1 Chronicles 16:11

Seek the Lord and his strength; seek his presence continually!

CHAPTER EIGHT

The Unveiling of Truth

When Jesus approached the Samaritan woman at the well, he embarked on a profound conversation that challenged her perceptions and revealed deep truths about herself. In the previous verses, we witnessed Jesus shattering social norms and engaging in dialogue with a Samaritan, a woman whom Jews would typically avoid. The significance of this encounter cannot be overstated, as it holds valuable lessons for each of us on our own journeys of self-discovery and spiritual growth.

As the conversation unfolded, Jesus offered the woman living water, a metaphorical representation of the eternal life and fulfillment that only God can provide. This invitation presented her with a choice, a pivotal moment where she had to confront the lies that had been imposed upon her by society and embrace the truth that she was worthy of God's love and grace. It is a familiar struggle that many of us face—believing the negative narratives others project onto us and allowing those falsehoods to dictate our self-perception.

Just when the woman was ready to accept this life-giving water, Jesus posed an unexpected request: "Go call your husband and then come back." This seemingly random demand held a purpose that transcended the surface level. Jesus knew her past and present circumstances intimately, and he gently exposed the truth she had kept hidden. In acknowledging her five husbands and the man she currently lived with, Jesus demonstrated his understanding and compassion, assuring her that he saw her as she truly was, beyond societal labels and judgments.

Through this revelation, Jesus emphasized a crucial lesson for all of us. It is not our external circumstances or societal roles that define us before God; rather, it is the state of our hearts and the authenticity of our worship. The woman, recognizing Jesus as a prophet, raised a question regarding the proper place of worship—whether on Mount Gerizim or in Jerusalem. In response, Jesus proclaimed that the time was coming when physical locations would no longer matter. Instead, true worship would be characterized by a genuine pursuit of truth, an engagement of the spirit, and an honest expression of our true selves before God.

The woman, though deeply affected by Jesus' words, still grappled with doubts and uncertainty. In many ways, she exemplified the complexity of belief and unbelief coexisting within an individual. Yet, Jesus persisted in his mission to bring her to a place of complete trust and faith. He understood the battle raging within her—the clash between the truth he presented and the weight of her past. He remained patient and steadfast, engaging in a lengthy conversation to convince her that, regardless of her history, she was deserving of salvation and a renewed hope in God.

This story serves as a powerful reminder that our perception of ourselves and the beliefs we hold are often influenced by external factors. The opinions, judgments, and expectations of others can shape our identity, leading us away from the truth of whom we are meant to be. Yet, Jesus invites us to break free from these constraints, to embrace the living water that quenches our deepest thirst, and to find our true selves in worship and adoration before God.

Just as the Samaritan woman found herself standing in her own way due to her self-perception, we too may find ourselves hindered by the lies we have internalized. But the encounter at the well reveals the transformative power of truth and the relentless pursuit of God's love. Jesus knew the woman's past, he exposed it, and yet, he offered her the gift of salvation without hesitation. In his eyes, her history did not define her worthiness or her ability to receive God's grace.

As we journey toward self-discovery and spiritual growth, let us heed the lessons from the woman at the well. May we recognize that the enemy seeks to manipulate our thoughts and feelings, binding us spiritually. But when we choose to engage with our true selves and embrace the truth that God sees in us, we become empowered to break free from the chains of doubt and self-imposed limitations. In that liberation, we find the strength to step into the fullness of whom we were created to be, accepting God's love and grace with open hearts.

The conversation at the well serves as a powerful testament to the transformative nature of encountering truth and embracing our true selves before God. It is an invitation to let go of the lies that have held us captive and to walk boldly in the freedom and hopes that Jesus offers.

As the conversation at the well continued, the Samaritan woman's initial skepticism and doubt began to transform into curiosity and openness. Jesus had skillfully addressed her past, gently exposing the truth while simultaneously assuring her of his understanding and acceptance. This revelation stirred within her a hunger for deeper understanding and connection.

With newfound eagerness, the woman acknowledged Jesus as a prophet and shared her knowledge of the Messiah who was to come. She eagerly awaited the day when all would be revealed. Little did she know that the one she was conversing with at that very moment was the long-awaited Messiah—the fulfillment of her hopes and the answer to her deepest longings.

Jesus, fully aware of the significance of the moment, responded to her anticipation. He declared, "I, the one speaking to you—I am he." At that moment, her eyes were opened, and she beheld the Messiah standing before her.

Overwhelmed by the encounter and the truth revealed, the woman's perspective shifted. No longer burdened by the weight of societal expectations or her past mistakes, she recognized the divine presence in her midst. Her encounter with Jesus at the well ignited a profound transformation within her.

Filled with awe and newfound understanding, the woman left her water jar behind and hurried back to the town. She became a living testament to the transformative power of encountering Jesus and embracing the truth. Bursting with excitement, she shared her encounter with the townspeople, exclaiming, "Come, see a man who told me everything I ever did. Could this be the Messiah?"

As the townspeople listened to her testimony and witnessed her transformed spirit, curiosity ignited within them. They too were drawn to encounter Jesus and discover the truth for themselves. The woman's encounter with Jesus had a ripple effect, spreading the message of hope and salvation throughout the town.

In this remarkable story, we witness the power of truth to liberate and transform. The Samaritan woman's journey from skepticism to belief serves as an invitation to each of us. It invites us to confront the lies and misconceptions that have held us captive, to embrace our true selves before God, and to experience the profound transformation that comes through encountering Jesus.

Like the Samaritan woman, we may have carried the weight of our past mistakes, allowing them to define us and hinder our relationship with God. But Jesus, in his boundless love and grace, longs to free us from the chains of self-condemnation and invite us into a life of purpose and fulfillment.

The story of the woman at the well challenges us to examine our own beliefs about ourselves and the narratives we have internalized. It urges us to let go of the limitations imposed by others and to embrace the truth of our identity as beloved children of God.

As we journey through life, may we remember the transformative power of encountering truth. Let us be open to the divine encounters that come our way, allowing them to shape our understanding of ourselves, our relationship with God, and our interactions with others. May we, like the Samaritan woman, become messengers of hope and transformation, sharing the truth we have encountered with those around us.

Chapter Takeaways

Chapter Takeaways

Affirmations

I embrace all the negative and positive aspects of my journey to greatness.

I will remain a profound, powerful soul for the remainder of my life.

My happiness is not tied to my ability to collect material objects or

achieve any particular goal, I am a brilliant being just for being here.

Scripture Reference

Psalms 73:26 26

My flesh and my heart may fail, but God is the strength of my heart and my portion forever.

CHAPTER NINE

Walking In Truth

It is in this new state that I speak of that God can use us. I want to encourage you today to really dive deep into yourself. I had to make a decision not to live any longer in a false reality. That false reality was the lies that came as a result of the experiences I had. There are so many things that I learned about myself along the way, but the process of finding me, just with the limited number of truths you read in this book, has transformed my mind and my walk with God as you wouldn't believe.

When I was going through failed relationships, I didn't realize that many weren't working because I couldn't give my all to the relationship. How could I? I was still in hiding. I was still protecting myself. Today, I understand that the journey to self-discovery is a process that is different for many, but taking the first step and admitting you don't truly know yourself is the first step. Giving up on whom you tried to build yourself up to be is the next step.

When I was in my doctoral program before I started, the counselor told me that if I were going to be successful, I would need to forget everything I knew and be open. I didn't understand what that meant at the time, but as I started the program, it made more sense. Coming into an area of study with the goal to add more knowledge can only be effective if it's not tainted by our own biases. It's natural to have beliefs, but we also learned that our beliefs, though we may feel strongly about them, are often manipulated by our experiences. In order for me to truly be successful in life and become who I am called to be, I need to continue to discover truths about myself.

God calls me blessed, he calls me the head and not the tail, he calls me a conqueror. Despite what I have been through, God's word never changes. I had to learn to look past my feelings and feed myself what God was saying about me, even when it didn't make sense. He is my creator and my lifeline. I found him. I'm growing in him. He has introduced me to myself, and I'm proud to say I am confidently walking in his truth of who I am today.

IIn this journey of self-discovery, I had to let go of the expectations I had for myself. I had built up an image of who I thought I should be based on societal standards, personal desires, and the opinions of others. But in the process of uncovering the layers that concealed my true self, I realized that the only expectation that truly mattered was the one God had for me. It was liberating to release the burden of trying to fit into a mold that was never meant for me.

Through prayer, reflection, and seeking wisdom, I began to uncover the unique qualities and gifts that God had placed within me. I embraced my strengths and acknowledged my weaknesses, knowing that in my weaknesses, God's strength is made perfect. I understood that my purpose in life was not defined by worldly success or external validation, but rather by how faithfully I lived out the calling God had placed on my life.

As I dug deeper into my identity in Christ, I discovered that my worth was not determined by my accomplishments or failures. It was rooted in the fact that I was fearfully and wonderfully made by a loving Creator. God's unconditional love and grace became the foundation on which I built my self-worth, knowing that I was accepted and cherished just as I am.

Through this process, I learned the power of vulnerability and authenticity. I realized that it was okay to be imperfect, to make mistakes, and to acknowledge my shortcomings. In fact, it was through embracing my vulnerabilities that I found true strength. It was in my brokenness that God's healing and restoration took place, transforming my weaknesses into testimonies of his faithfulness.

Day by day, I continue to grow and evolve, guided by the truth that resides within me. It is an ongoing journey of self-discovery, as I unravel the layers of conditioning, societal expectations, and personal fears. I am no longer confined by the limitations I once placed upon myself. Instead, I walk in the freedom of knowing that I am fearfully and wonderfully made, destined for a purpose greater than myself.

IIn this new state of self-discovery, I am able to fully surrender to God's plan for my life. I trust in his divine guidance and rely on his strength to navigate the challenges that come my way. I am no longer afraid to step out of my comfort zone, for I know that God is with me every step of the way.

As you embark on your own journey of self-discovery, I encourage you to embrace the process. Be open to uncovering the truths that lie within you. Release the false realities and expectations that hold you back, and instead, lean into the unconditional love and acceptance of your heavenly Father. Remember, you are fearfully and wonderfully made, and your life has a purpose that only you can fulfill. Trust in God's plan, and allow him to guide you on the path to becoming the person he has created you to be.

As you continue on your journey of self-discovery, there may be moments of doubt and uncertainty. You may face setbacks and encounter obstacles along the way. But do not be discouraged, for these are opportunities for growth and transformation. Embrace them as part of the process and trust that God is using them to shape you into the person He desires you to be.

Seek out wisdom and guidance from those who have walked a similar path. Surround yourself with supportive and encouraging individuals who believe in your potential. Share your experiences and learn from others who have embraced their true selves. Together, you can inspire and uplift one another, creating a community of authenticity and acceptance.

As you delve deeper into your true identity, remember to be patient and kind to yourself. Self-discovery is a lifelong journey, and it is okay to take the time you need to explore different aspects of your being. Give yourself permission to make mistakes and learn from them. Celebrate the small victories and milestones along the way, for each step forward is a testament to your growth and resilience.

During this process, you may uncover passions, talents, and dreams that have been dormant within you. Embrace these newfound revelations and pursue them with courage and determination. Allow yourself to explore new opportunities and step outside of your comfort zone. Remember, true fulfillment lies in living a life aligned with your authentic self and utilizing your unique gifts to make a positive impact in the world.

As you grow in your understanding of who you are, never forget the importance of your relationship with God. He is the ultimate source of your identity and purpose. Seek His guidance through prayer, meditate on His word, and cultivate a deep and intimate connection with Him. In His presence, you will find strength, clarity, and the unwavering love that will sustain you throughout your journey.

In conclusion, the path of self-discovery is an awe-inspiring and transformative journey. It is a process of shedding the layers that conceal your true self and embracing the person God has created you to be. Embrace the challenges, celebrate the victories, and trust in the divine plan that unfolds before you. As you embark on this journey, may you find solace in the knowledge that you are not alone, for God is with you every step of the way, guiding you towards a life of purpose, fulfillment, and authenticity.

Chapter Takeaways

Chapter Takeaways

Affirmations

What are you affirming over your life today???

Scripture Reference

Luke 10:16 "Whoever listens to you listens to me; whoever rejects you rejects me; but whoever rejects me rejects him who sent me."

Made in the USA
Columbia, SC
18 June 2023